James Grahame

Poems in English, Scotch, and Latin

James Grahame

Poems in English, Scotch, and Latin

ISBN/EAN: 9783337005993

Printed in Europe, USA, Canada, Australia, Japan

Cover: Foto ©Thomas Meinert / pixelio.de

More available books at **www.hansebooks.com**

POEMS,

IN

ENGLISH, SCOTCH, *and* LATIN.

Majores majora fonent; mihi parva locuto
Sufficit in veftras fæpe redire manus.

MART.

PAISLEY:

PRINTED BY J. NEILSON, FOR THE AUTHOR.

1794.

PREFACE.

I HAVE now, gentle Reader, arrived at that ſtage, of an *Author's progreſs*, where Dedications, and Prefaces, and Mottos, and half-length Prints of the Author come to be thought of. Dedications I hate. They are in general compounds of lies and flattery; and beſides, I have no friends among the great. I have ſeveral in the leſs conſpicuous (for I do not call them the *inferior)* orders of life : but I am averſe to involve them in any ſhare of that mortification to which, perhaps, my preſent attempt will ſubject me. As to the half-length Print of the Au-thor,—were I to behold my figure ſtuck up as a frontiſpiece to this vo-lume, I ſhould be apt to conſider my-ſelf as expoſed on a kind of pillory, with the Title-page by way of Label to denote my crime, and the Poems themſelves as the *Corpus delicti* hung round my neck.

For theſe weighty reaſons I have determined neither to expoſe my friend

in a dedication, nor myself in a print:
and for others, equally weighty, I have
resolved to write this Preface.

Without further preface, then, to the
preface,---I think it proper to mention,
by way of apology, such as it is, for
the many defects observable in the
following Poems, that the only cor-
rections which they have received, are
such as my own judgment has suggest-
ed. So little indeed have I been guilty
of shewing or reciting my verses to
friends, (the common vice of poetasters)
that I am scarcely indebted to any body for a single hint or advice.

I fhall perhaps be accufed of pre-
fumption, in offering a book to the
public view, without having taken the
advantage of private criticifm and cor-
rection. The truth is,—inconfiftent as
it may feem with my prefent teme-
rity—I never had the face to afk any
one to undertake the embarraffing,
and almoft incompatible offices of
Critic and Friend.

Perhaps too, fome fmall degree of
malevolent perfonality will be imput-
ed to me. I anfwer, that I have not
attacked any characters but fuch as
are either notorioufly profligate, or un-
principled, or avaricious. I have been

ftimulated, not by malevolence, but indignation;

Si natura negat, facit indignatio verfum.

JUVENAL.

My attempts in Latin Verfe I fubmit to the perufal of the learned (if I may hope for that honour) with the utmoft hefitation and diffidence. I have already, from time to time, difcovered feveral metrical errors; and I am afraid fome may have ftill efcaped my obfervation. What adds to my apprehenfion on this head, is, that I have been obliged to depend folely and entirely on my own accuracy; for I am not in habits of intimacy with a single perfon who underftands the mechanifm of Latin verfe half fo well as myfelf.

With regard to the Imitations of Horace, I may anticipate an obvious criticifm ; namely, that there is much of the *travefti* in them. I own that there is, and fay—fo much the better.—The drefs, which I have chofen for them, is the broad Scottifh dialect ; and it appears here, I flatter myfelf, in more purity, with more of the true Scottifh idiom, and with a fmaller mixture of Englifh, than in moft other performances that pafs under the name of *Poems in the Scottifh dialect.*

And now, gentle Reader, if after perufing the following little volume, or any part of it, thou fhouldft find thyfelf more difpofed to condemn than approve, pronounce fentence, I befeech thee, with as little afperity as the nature of the offence feems to merit. Thunder not forth the harfh epithets ----blockhead, fool, puppy, upon my offending head-----or ftupid, quaint, childifh, againft my harmlefs book. Confider that, if I have written *invita Minerva*, the lofs has been my own : if with her affent, ftill my Pegafus

B

(like the Tròjan horſe) is at beſt the

————" donum *exitiale* Minervæ."

VIRG.

CONTENTS.

IMITATIONS AND TRANSLATIONS.

VERSES IN LATIN.

ERRATA.

P. 22. l. 1. For *wit,* read *with.*

32. 7. For *thou,* read *thee.*

103. 5. For *frien's,* read *friens.*

104. 5. For *defcendere,* read *difcedere.*

7. For the fecond *quid,* read *quis.*

112. For *Sapho,* read *Sappho.*

P O E M S.

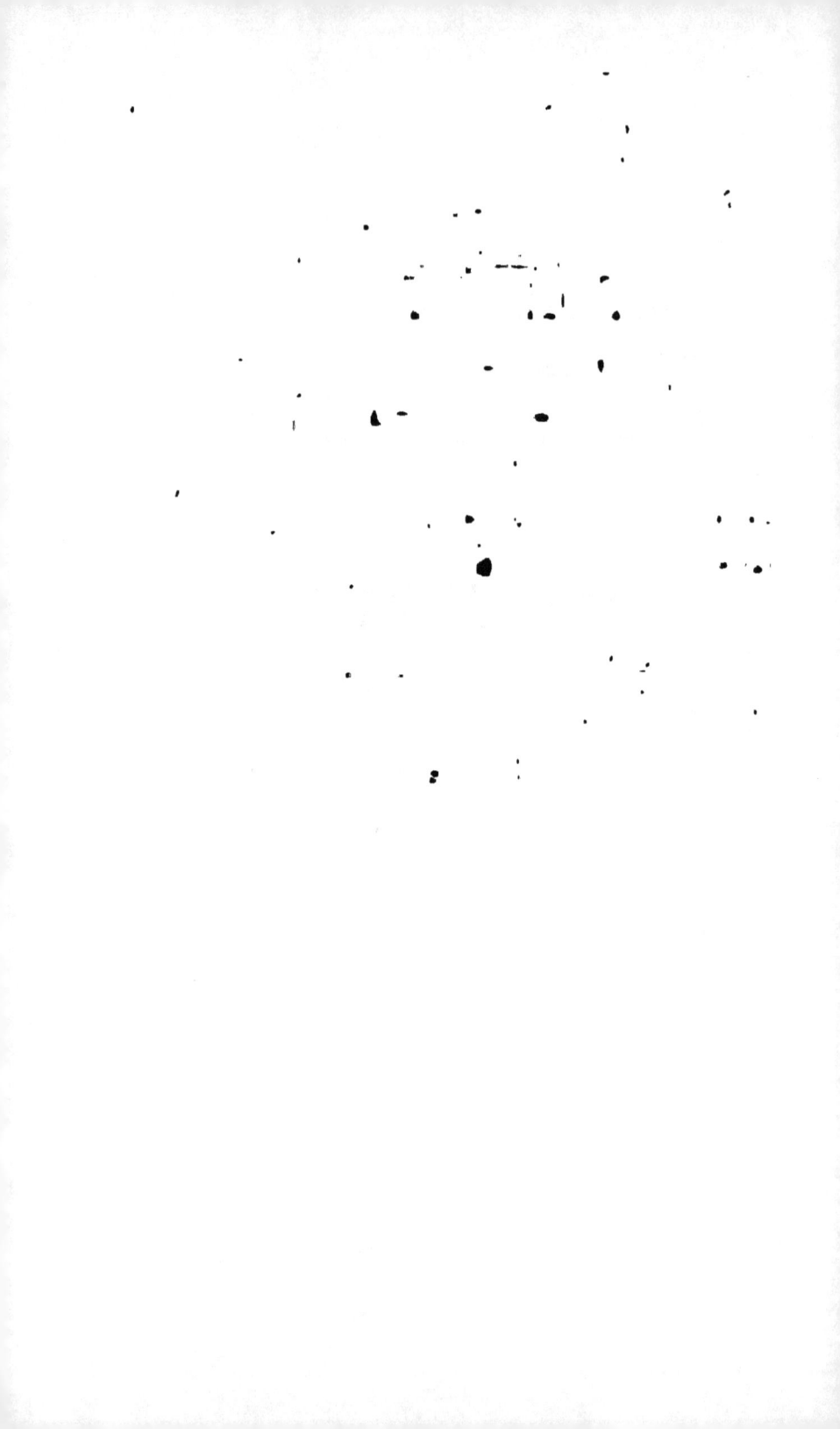

SPRING.

T HE hill, the dale, the woodland, and the ftream,
Of various bards have been th' unvaried theme.
If then, of hill, dale, wood, and ftream I write,
Will not the fated reader cry—'Tis trite?
The field is reap'd I muft, alas, admit;
But ftill the laws of God and Man permit
The gleaner, following the reaper band,
To fill with fcatter'd ears his meagre hand.—
To rural fcenes I raife my feeble voice:
O were my life thus fubject to my choice!

If heaven my weary hopes fhould ever crown
With leave to fly the bufy buftling town,
In Scottifh glen low fhall my dwelling ftand,
With tangling woods and fhallow brooks at hand,

C

And garden fenc'd with hedge of eglantine
And hawthorn interfpers'd with fweet woodbine:
My roof not high, my parlour warm and clean,
With windows fmall, and learned fhelves between,
Where Cowper, Barbauld, Burns may find a place,
And even Virgil dare to fhew his face:
A cottage, not a caftle, is my prayer;
O may't not be a cottage in the air!
And you, to whom the real blifs belongs,
While I but clafp the fhadow in my fongs,
Learn, nor defpife inftruction tho' in rhyme,.
How to enjoy, not kill the fleeting time.

When April ftrews the woods with primrofe flowers,
When oft the day is dimm'd with hovering fhowers,
When cuckoo birds repeat th' unchanging fong,
And muddy rivers fluggifh fteal along,—
The wat'ry wiles now long difus'd prepare,
Unloofe the ravell'd line with patient care,

Fix well the hook, then dip the faplefs wand,
And throw the line athwart with waving hand.
Slowly it glides down with the dufky flood,
Bearing along the fatal treacherous food.
It finks—it finks again—but do not pull;
'Tis but the nibbling of fome fportive fool:
Wait cautious till the floating fignal dive,
Now gently pull, O do not rafhly ftrive;
The flender wand to every motion bends,
And yielding, in a drooping crefcent ends:
Soon on the bank the ftruggling captive lies,
Then in the wicker prifon gafping dies.

But if thy fkill fuch humble fport deride,
Wait until when the fwollen ftreams fubfide,
Till when the fwallows fkim along the flood
And flitting zig-zag catch the infect brood.
O'er night the mimic flies arrange with care,
The brown, the gray, the gilded, and the fair,

With earlieſt dawn up from thy ſlumbers ſpring,

Ere yet the morning birds begin to ſing:

And O leave not behind th' unweeting boy,

Nor cheat him dreaming of the promis'd joy;

Go rouſe him gently, ſee him ſleeping ſmile,

Then, if thou canſt, his wak'ning hopes beguile:

Thy ſteps he'll follow grateful and ſubmiſs,

Study thy looks, and fear to do amiſs.

But feigning angry mien, and wrathful tone,

Command the rambling ſpaniel to be gone;

Then lightly ſkiff along the dewy plain,

Until the miſty river's ſide you gain.

If there ſucceſs you wiſh, obſerve this rule,—

Where ends the ſtream and where begins the pool,

Let the wing'd lure among the eddies play

And dancing round delude the ſpeckled prey.

Beware—be not impatiently raſh,

Nor fretfully the harmleſs ſurface laſh;

The limber line with wary motion throw,

Let it fall gently like a flake of ſnow,

Which filent melts as on the ftream it lights
And with the wat'ry element unites :
And ftill be mindful of the heedlefs eye
Of the fmall wight who playful fitteth nigh.
So fhall your arts a noble prize delude,
So the huge trout fhall fnatch the feeming food.
See how he fhoots along ftretching the line :
Indulge his way, do not his force confine.
Fainter and fainter efforts ftill are try'd,
Till on the ftream floats his enamell'd fide ;
Pulled flow afhore, he pants with frequent gafp,
And dyes the little hands that fcarce around him clafp

'Neath flood-fcoop'd rocks, and thro' deep track-
lefs dells,
Where fairies haunt, (as village rumour tells)
Where oft is heard the boding fcreech-owl's fcream,
Upward you trace the flowly leffening ftream.
Begins the fun now downward to defcend,
Now more and more the trees their fhades extend :

Tir'd of fuccefs, and loaded wit the fpoil,
Homeward acrofs the furrow'd fields you toil.
Your watchful dog afar your coming fpies,
Soon at your feet the crouching fuppliant lies.

If to the ftreams one day you thus allot,
The two that follow to the Mufe devote:
Lift to the fong of the Mæonian fwan,
The fall of Troy, the much-enduring Man
Who wrought her fall: or, if the Mantuan ftrain
In pleafing rapture all your foul detain,
Blefs bounteous Heaven that form'd you to enjoy
Pleafures fo pure, pleafures without alloy.
But long in fields of fiction do not rove,
Nor always lounge in the poetic grove:
Let tales of real life your mind engage,
And fearch for truth in the hiftoric page.

While yet 'tis fpring, I to the tardy team
Refort full oft, and fee the ploughfhare gleam;

With clay-clogg'd feet cumber'd I walk along,
Beneath the muſic of the Laverok's ſong,
The while the ſower ſteps, with waving hand
And loaded ſheet, along the furrow'd land.

SUMMER.

PALE primrofes among the woods decay,
And hyacinths bedeck fweet fmiling May;
The blackbird chaunts upon the full blown thorn,
And all the woodland chorus cheers the morn.
Now to the dewy hill direct thy way,
The varied plain with grateful eye furvey,
And view the windings of the hidden ftream,
Where mifty wreaths lurk from the rifing beam.
Behold the diftant city's fmoky fhroud,
Where dim-feen fpires peep thro' the brooding cloud:
Compare thy lot with theirs who yonder toil,
Whofe life is one inceffant fore turmoil,
Who only once in feven long days inhale,
In fhort excurfion, the cool weftern gale.
For me—how feldom are my wifhes crown'd
With leave to fly the ftunning, dizzying found!

And when indulg'd, how fleeting the fojourn!

How foon by whifpering care urg'd to return!

The captive bird, thus from the cage fet free,

Flies to the grove and flits from tree to tree;

Each dell, each bofky bourne he loves to range,

Rejoicing in the life-renewing change:

But all unus'd to feek the woodland fare,

Or to endure the midnight's chilling air,

Back to his prifon—he forfakes the wood,

And, ah! too common, freedom fells for food.

While yet the dew-drop glifters in the fhade,

Ere yet the fun-beams reach the hidden glade,

The aged labourer quits his morning toil,

His well-worn fpade fix'd in th' inverted foil.

Afar his little boy, pleas'd he defcries,

Who light of heart faft from the village hies;

In this hand hangs a fcrip, in that a pail,

The frugal difhes of his parent's meal:

The fimple viands on the grafs are fpread,

The fire uncovers flow his hoary head,

And grateful to his God and Father pays

His humble homage and unfeigned praife,—

To him who to the ravens gave command

To feed his fervant in the defert land.

This man had fought in fields beftrewn with dead,

And in his thanklefs country's caufe had bled,—

For them who roll in eafe without one thought

Of all the woe with which that eafe is bought;

Who gorge remorfelefs at the coftly feaft

What would a ftarving family make bleft;

Who feize the widow's mite when in arrear,

Stern and relentlefs to the pleading tear,

Then, if they give a tefter to the poor,

Believe the generous deed will heaven fecure;

And think that what thus to the Lord is lent

Will be repaid with intereft cent. per cent.—

Ye fordid, pitiful, low. grovelling things,

Go grind the poor, go lick the duft to kings.

Refiftlefs heat broods o'er the thirfty plains;

Among the woods a liftlefs filence reigns;

The drooping bird no longer loves to fing,

But quits the branch and laves its fluttering wing;

The beggar leaves the road, embrown'd with duft,

And in the fhaded fountain foaks his cruft:

To the hoarfe-babbling brook the poet ftrays,

Or loves to lofe himfelf far 'mid the greenwood's

    maze.

Let me the river's dazzling glare avoid,

And lay me on the ftreamlet's fhady fide,

So narrow on the farther bank I fee

Humming from flower to flower the devious bee,

While grafhoppers, with intermitting voice,

Raife all around a feeble, chirping noife.

THE

MINOR POETS.

POETS!— to what fhall I refemble 'em ?
The Cuckoo is their proper emblem.
While other birds are building nefts
Her idle windpipe never refts.
Like her, without or houfe or home,
The vagrant race of Poets roam.
Like her their fav'rite theme is fpring,
'Tis then they make the vallies ring,
Hers too's a fleeting fhort-liv'd lay,
The Poet's feldom lafts a day ;
And there's as much (believe a brother)
Variety in one as t'other.

ESSAY ON DOG,

Part Firſt.

ARGUMENT.

Invocation addreſſed to Pompey—Of Dog in the Abſtract—The Maſtiff—The Shepherd's Dog—The Town Dog—The Pointer.

" Awake my St. John, leave all meaner things
" To low ambition, and the pride of Kings."

POPE's Eſſay on Man.

AWAKE, my Pompey, ſhake thy pliant ears,
And liſten to my ſong, a ſong of thee,
And of Dogkind. Enough has now been ſung
By man, that egotiſt, himſelf the theme.
An humbler ſubject for my ſtrains I chuſe,
Strains unadorn'd with harmony of rhyme:
I ſing the poor man's never-changing friend,

The friend still true when all have turn'd their back;
If prosperous his lot, submissive still,
Or if adverse, not knowing to repine;
Content whether he eat the rich man's bread,
Or the blind beggar lead from door to door.
Mistaken man, thou call'st thy foe *a dog*,——
This his suppos'd reproach, his greatest praise.
If dogs in language could their thoughts impart,
Mayhap they'd call a vicious cur—*a man*.
Nor think the difference great 'twixt thee and him:
Like man, " he reasons not contemptibly ;"
He loves, he hates, he robs, he steals,
And, had he gift of speech, perhaps he'd lie.
Yea, too, full oft he pisseth 'gainst the wall,
Ancient criterion of the human kind *.
And as in characters of men is seen
Diversity of shades, so 'tis in Dogs,
From the huge house-dog to the lap-dog small.

Close by his box the sent'nel mastiff lies :

* 1 Kings xvi. 11.

His head couch'd 'twixt his paws he fcarcely deigns
To turn, but rolls his fcowling eyes afkance;
The quaking paffenger, affuming looks
Of carelefs boldnefs, fearful moves along,
But fudden at the fmalleft growl he ftarts;
The monfter ftrives to break his rattling chain;
Poor flave! by flav'ry render'd ftill more fierce.

Fam'd for a race of dogs are Tweed's blythe braes
And hills green to the fummit. Sweetly there
The fhepherd tunes his reed to Scotia's lays,
Until the downward fun has left the glens
Tinging the mountain tops; then at a word
His faithful dog, cautious, with circuit wide,
Wears in the ftraying flock. They to the fold
Wend leifurely along, where fafe fhut in,
With gate that erft had harrow'd fruitful fields,
Old now and of its teeth difarm'd, peaceful they reft.
O happy you, the happieft of your kind,

Ye fhepherds dogs! if ye but knew your blifs *.

What, Luath, tho' thy fare be fcant and poor,

Tho' at the good-wife's churn thou'rt fain to watch,

And lick the frothy drops that fall around :

Yet peace fecure, and fleep in fun or fhade,

And hill and dale, and wood, and ftream are thine.

Far happier thou, I ween, than city cur.

No knavifh boys delude thee with a cruft,

Whilft to thy tail they fix the rattling pan :

And when old age fhall cripple all thy joints,

Thou'lt not be fet adrift to fteal for food,

Like the poor negro-flave outcaft and helplefs ;

Nor from the bridge, with ftone hung round thy neck,

Wilt thou by unrelenting hand be thrown.

---

* O fortunatos nimium fua fi bona norint
Agricolas! —— —— ——————
At fecura quies, et nefcia fallere vita,
Dives opum variarum; at latis otia fundis,
Speluncæ, vivique lacus; at frigida tempe,
Mugitufque boum, mollefque fub arbore fomni
Non abfunt !

VIRG. Gcor. II.

Of dog and man the depth of mifery
In cities ftill is found. Oft have I feen,
On wintry morn, in tatter'd weeds a wretch
Picking the cinders from the dunghill heaps,
And fhivering at the felf-fame fpot her dog
Scraping for bones; when happy if he find
The wifh'd-for prize, fearful he fkulks away
And in fome hidden nook enjoys the feaft,
Unlefs perchance, growling with tufks difplay'd
Some ftronger pirate meet him by the way,
And feize the morfel from his trembling jaw.

What tho' with blinding fnows the fhepherd's dog
Muft ftruggle oft, driving the famifh'd flock
Round from the fatal fhelter of the hill,
Where wreaths on wreaths fmooth up the trea-
     cherous glen:
At night his toils are o'er; and bafking warm
Before the blazing fire he dries his jetty coat.

E

See o'er the ftubble ridge the Pointer range:

This way and that he traverfes the field.

Sudden with eager look and cautious ftep

Couring he creeps, till ftiffen'd all at once,

With lifted foot quite motionlefs he ftands.

The fpoɽtfman onward moves with throbbing heart.

Down comes the whirring pinion to the ground.

But barbarous joys delight me now no more;

Fly rather, Pompey, to my Delia's bowers;

Say, does fhe fmiling take thy proffer'd paw,

Nor chide thee, tho' thou foil her fnow-white ftole,

Stroaking with gentle hand thy fpotted head?

       *   *   *   *   *

POET'S ADDRESS

TO HIS NEW BOOK.

I'VE thrown thee, friend, into the ſtream of fame;
To ſink or ſwim depends all on thyſelf.
O may'ſt thou, as th' Orphean lyre of old,
When gliding down th Iſmenian river's ſtream,
Call forth the echoes from their twilight grots,
And make the banks thy melody reſound.
May ne'er thy page be injur'd by the flood,
But like the ſwan's fair breaſt remain undrench'd,
As rowing down the ſilver tide he charms
With ſweeteſt raviſhment the liſtening woods.

Still be thy fate as various as thy theme,—
Read by the rich, the poor, the high, the low,
The grave, the gay, the polifh'd, and the rude;
One while in hands as fair as was thy leaf
Ere yet my Mufe had ftain'd it with her fcrawl;
  Anon foil'd by fome fagely-fnuffing fool,
Mayhap befprinkled by his boifterous fneeze.

  Chiefly to youth and beauty pay thy court,
And competence ftill willing to be pleafed:
And, while I ftruggle thro' the juftling crowd,
Be thou at eafe reclin'd with brother bards
In parlour fnug, far from the dufty fhelf.
And, O! what tranfport would it be to think,
That, like the fong of the Mæonian bard
Beneath the conquering Macedonian's head,
Thou all below th' Elyfian pillow lay
Of her, whofe eyes more lafting conquefts gain
Than did the furious fword of Ammon's fon!
Or—may fhe leaning on fome flowery bank,

With fweet approving eye fhine on thy page,

And, when fhe clofeth' thee, fold 'twixt thy leaves,

The primrofe pale or purple violet,

To mark the page reluctant which fhe left.

Ah me! how vain are thefe afpiring hopes!

Perhaps to fervile purpofes thou deftin'd art;

And 'ftead of lighting flames in Delia's breaft,

Thou'lt only light her taper when fhe reads

Some hated rival's more engaging lay:

Perhaps a fate even ftill more vile awaits,—

To clean the fuds from off the razor's edge;

To wad the cruel murderous fowling-piece;

Or damn'd to heaven thou'lt foar a paper kite;

Or blaze a funeral pile for fingeing fowls.

If then, the paper, not the verfe is priz'd,

Go, happy, twift my Delia's lovely locks,

And in her ringlets bound kifs that fweet neck,

That galaxy of every grace divine.

FRAGMENTS

OF A POEM ON DUELLING.

SAY, Mufe, what caufe fo forcible can make one
Expofe to powder and to ball one's bacon?
For my poor part, I fay, and always faid,
That 'tis the fear of being thought afraid.
What mighty folly to avenge the pains
Of trampled toe, at peril of one's brains!
How impious in mortal man to fcatter
The facred contents of his *Pia mater!*
But what my patience drives to the *ne plus*
Ultra, and would were I the man of Uz,
Is to confider that the fawning wretch
To whom fome Lordling calls—go—carry—fetch,—

The powder'd, perfum'd, pimping, prating varlet,
Prefuming on cockade and coat of fcarlet,
The flufter'd coward, wifhing to retrieve
The honour, which in battle he did leave,
By *honour's* laws may force the *man of Rofs*
To ftake his Sterling worth againft their drofs;
Or that fome ruin'd gambler, to avoid
The trouble and the crime of fuicide,
The beft of men with infult may provoke
At once to give and to receive the ftroke.

In gambling annals, was there ever known
The rich man's purfe againft the poor one's thrown
Quite by the flump?—Since then 'tis always found,
When money's rifk'd, that pound is ftak'd 'gainft
          pound,
Shilling 'gainft fhilling, pennies againft pence,
Where's the confiftency with common fenfe,
That when *life's* ftak'd, all thought of worth's omitted,
And with a patriot a ftate fwindler pitted?—

When,—merit weigh'd,—the odds were fairly laid
Were Charles' curl rifk'd 'gainft Billy's head.

* * * * * * * * *

And now behold depart on pious miffion
Yond B ——— p vowing 'gainft his foes perdition,
Swearing by blood and wounds, hell-fire and
    thunder,
That with the voice of four and twenty pounder
He'll foon convert the atheiftic tribe,
Make them the Athanafian creed fubfcribe,
Force them *Te Deum* on their knees to bellow,
And for their daily bread a wafer fwallow.

* * *

In order to prevent any mifconftruction of thefe laft lines, it may be proper to mention, that they were written with no view of conveying any reflection againft *religion*, but folely with the view of expofing the wickednefs and folly of attempting by force of arms, to re-eftablifh a *fuperftition*, the abfurdity, nonfenfe, and blafphemy of which, joined with the ignorance, bigotry, cruelty, profligacy, atheifm, tyranny, and rapacity of its priefts, have driven almoft a whole nation to infidelity.

REDBREAST.

To him who wades thro' autumn's leaf-ftrewn
    paths,
Ere long to be as deep o'erlaid with fnow,
Sweetly the Redbreaft mourns the parting year,
Sweetly with woodland melody he foothes
The favage breaft of man, his future hoft.
When falcon Winter hovers o'er the wood
He flies for refuge to the haunts of men;
Firft to the trim-built ftack or bufy barn;
But foon as Boreas drives along the plain
With fnow and blinding fleet, nearer he draws,
And from the window pecks the fprinkled crumbs;
Till bolder grown, as fiercer drifts the ftorm,

F

Within th' expecting threfhold he alights,

" And pays to trufted man his annual vifit."

Oft have I feen thee, in my boyifh days,

(Ere yet I knew the city's vain turmoil)

Perch'd on the diftaff of the houfemaid's wheel :

She fung of lovers faithlefs, maids undone,

Of faithful lovers, and of faithlefs feas,

Thy notes with her's in artlefs concert join'd.

Did ever fchool-boy rob poor Redbreaft's houfe?

No fure : for well each thoughtlefs truant knows,

'Twas this fweet bird that left his neft half built,

And carrying leaf by leaf, from morn to eve,

Enwrapt the children in the wood forlorn,

All with a fragrant fhroud. At thought of this

The fpoiler's outftretch'd eager hand recoils,

Softly on tiptoe, hufh, he fteals away,

The dam affiduous fits, nor leaves her charge.

BURNS,

THE SCOTTISH POET.

> " Ilk happing bird, wee helplefs thing,
> " That in the merry months of fpring
> " Delighted me to hear thee fing,
>   " What comes o' thee ?
> " Whare doft thou cowr thy chittering wing
>   " Or clofe thy ee ?"
>
> *A Winter Night.*—BURNS.

THE bard whofe fong ftill echoes in the vale,

The bard whofe fong each lovely tongue recites,

Is left to moil like men of common mould ;

The fong ftill charms us ; but the bard's forgot.

'Tis thus the thrufh, fweet minftrel of the fpring,

His woodnotes wild pours from the milk-white thorn ;

But when ftern Winter chills the leaflefs grove,

Shivering he's left to glean his fcanty food,
Nor ever is the woodland path beftrewn,
Save with intent to lure him to the fnare.

Ungrateful country! ill-requited Burns!
Shall he who fung, in Scotia's Doric lays,·
" The lowly train in life's fequefter'd fcene,"
Remain neglected in the fcene he paints,
And afk, perhaps in vain, " for leave to toil?"
Shall.he who fung far fweeter than the lark,
When upward fpringing from the daify's fide
To greet the purpling eaft,
Be driven from the fields cheer'd by his fong?
Who e'er with truth and yet with dignity
Like him rehears'd the annals of the poor?
Did e'er religion half fo lovely feem
In temples, as in his low lonely cot?
" The Power incens'd the pageant will defert,
" The pompous ftrain, the facerdotal ftole,
" And haply in fome cottage far apart

" May hear, well-pleas'd, the language of the foul;

" And in his book of life the inmates poor inrol."

Ye patrons of the mighty dead, who ftrive

T' immortalize immortal Thomfon's name,

Rear not to angels mole-hill monuments,

While living merit owns no fheltering roof:

Rather would Thomfon's gentle fpirit fee

A manfion rais'd for his neglected Burns,

Than gorgeous maufoleums for himfelf.

[Written feveral years ago.]

TO THE

MOON.

FAIR filver Moon, while I the live long night,
With fleeplefs eye gaze on thy pale-fac'd orb,
My thoughts on Delia fixt, thou, happy Moon!
Doft thro' her cafement fhine, and filent fteal
Kiffes from her unconfcious lovely lip.
Shine not fo bright, fweet Moon, thou'lt wake my
      love ;
Soft veil thee in a fleecy limber cloud,
So may'ft thou view her charms in fleep more charm-
      ing far,
Her eyes more beauteous now than when awake,
As flowers when fhut than fpreading to the fun.

TO

CARE.

SNUG in the covert hid the panting hare
Lays fear aſide and vainly thinks ſhe's ſafe;
But ſoon th' approaching noiſe ſwells in the gale:
So, Care, where'er I flee, cloſe thou purſu'ſt;
Thro' city, country, crowd or ſolitude;
Whether with wary ſtep, Edina fair,
Along thy fragrant ſtreet I cull my path
At morning hour; or o'er the miſty lawn
Bruſh thro' the gliſtering dew, and wake the lark;
Or penetrate at noon th' embowering wood.
Or if, (in happy but deluſive dreams)
With Delia's lovely hand faſt lock'd in mine,
I ſee reflected from th' unruffled brook
All-beauteous the wat'ry image ſmile,
Ev'n there thou thruſt'ſt thy lowring face between,
And bid'ſt us part.

TO

DELIA.

OUR old Scotch faints before a battle
Did with the Lord firft try their mettle
In prayer, (as the ftory goes)
To blefs themfelves and curfe their foes;
Nay with him were fo very daring
As venture wreftling and fparring,
And at the laft turn'd fo expert
I' th' fpiritual gymnaftic art,
That, laying by their ufelefs fwords,
They gain'd great victories by words.
Now if thofe blades durft with their Maker
Fight at pull, devil, and pull, baker,
Why may not I, O Goddefs fweet,
When bending fuppliant at thy feet,

When prayer and pennance nought avail,
When humble filence ftill doth fail,
At one great throw adventure all,
And with thee boldly try a fall?—

G

D——D H——E.

" DOUBT every thing," the fceptic cries;

" To men, to books, no faith is due:"—

His Hiftory's fo fill'd with *lies*,

It almoft proves his doctrine *true*.

UNANSWERABLE ARGUMENT

FOR THE SLAVE TRADE.

SAYS one to a merchant; " 'Tis furely a crime
" To fteal men, altho' from a tropical clime :—
" Yes, Sir," fays the Merchant, " we'll own you
  " are right,
" When once you've demonftrated black to be
  " white."

DEATH

OF A FRIEND.

LONG did he ftrive againft th' o'erwhelming
    ftorm,
Long bear diftrefs in every varied form:
Hufh'd were the waves at laft, calm was his death,
Peaceful in fleep he did refign his breath;
No watchful eye the parting moment knew,
Dreaming of heaven—he wak'd—the dream was true.

———————

" Vindex avaræ fraudis." Hor.

EPISTLE

FROM A

POOR BLIND COBLER TO A RICH CANDLE-MAKER.

Let your light fo fhine before men, that they may fee your good works
and glori.y your Father which is in Heaven.

Matt. chap. v. v. 16.

M OST reverend Sir, I'm truly vext
That you fhould counteract my text;
For tho' your works and candles fhine
With luftre glorious, yea divine,
Yet if folks eyes your bratlings blow out,
You may let one and t' other go out,
And henceforth and for ever ceafe
To dip in gofpel or in greafe.

Your generous offer, I muſt own,

Surpaſſed expecta-ti-on;

For when you ſaw me robb'd of ſight

You ſaid I ſhould not want for light,

And of complaint t' avoid all handle,

Agreed to give me coal and candle:

As for all other neceſſaries,

You knew the bounty of the pariſh.

You ſaid too, without any ſtickling,

You'd ſend me now and then ſome *crackling,*

Which, though by ſome thought only fit

For feeding watch-dog or turn-ſpit,

Is, I muſt own, quite good enough,

And of your charity ſtrong proof.

To charity I know you truſt

To ſave your bacon at the laſt:

You built a church. and ſerve the cure,

And rail againſt the ſcarlet whore.

But is not this to pleaſe your pride?

It is—the thing can't be denied:

You think it mighty fine to gabble
To a half-witted, crazy rabble.

You preach the gofpel to the poor,
Believing thus you'll heaven fecure,
Of fp'ritual food full liberal,
But fparing of the temporal.
Regardlefs of your time and pains
You ftuff and cram your hearers brains,
While their poor empty ftomachs grumble
With many a woful hollow rumble.
But know (ere long you'll know't too well)
That you may *build baith kirk and mill,*
May cant, and whine, exhort, and pray,
And yet be damn'd eternally.
Then, while you turn and tofs in limbo,
I'll fit and fmile with arms akimbo,
And when you afk a drop of water,
(You call this devilifh—no matter,)
I'll tell you tauntingly, go fwallow
A ladleful of boiling tallow.

———————

WISHES.

————————————————O ubi campi
Sperchiufque, et virginibus bacchata Lacænis
Taygeta! O qui me gelidis in vallibus Hæmi
Siſtat, et ingenti ramorum protegat umbra!

VIRG.

ONCE Virgil on a fultry day
Did thus the gods invoke and pray,
" O place me on the ſhady ſide
" Of Hæmus, elfe I ſhall be fry'd:
" Since Phaeton's days was never felt
" Such heat; the Devil's felf 'twould melt,
" The Dev'l who, like a falamander,
" Thro' flames with beard unfing'd doth wander."

1

When Phœbus' rays come down pell-mell,
Some modern bards figh for a well,
(In rhyming tongue yclep'd a fountain
Spouting from the breezy mountain;)
Some headlong rufh into the pool
Their fervid carcafes to cool.
Fair ladies long for Grampian fnows,
There to dance with breechlefs beaux;
Nay fome would wear the philabeg,
Nor blufh to fhew a fnow-white leg,
Nor grudge to grant a trifling favour
To the gently kifling zephyr,
Wer't not for tyrant Cuftom's laws,
Who rules the fex with iron paws.—
For me, tho' hot like Dives broiling,
Or a live lobfter fet a boiling,
No place there is I'd fooner pitch on,
Than that cool grot, Sir Jamie's kitchen;

H

THE

HISTORY OF J. B.

OR THE NEW METAMORPHOSIS.

Anfer in Hominem.

ACCORDING to Pythagoras's
Doctrine, fome men are chang'd to affes;
Geefe too are oft transform'd to men,
And men to geefe as oft again.
In proof of this there's B——s our friend,
A friend, tho' never known to lend.
His neck, which, like his purfe, is long,
Is now th' occafion of my fong.
This neck of his made fome rude fellows
Say, he had fure dropt from the gallows.

He to refute fuch calumnies,
(Which as you'll hear were all damn'd lies)
Relates his wondrous tranfmigration,
Of which I give you this narration.

He tells how once he was a fwan,
How next he was transform'd to man,
How that his collar ftill retains
Of 'ts ancient form fome faint remains.

He next unto his legs appeals,
Six inches fcarce 'twixt knee and heels:
And if his hearers ftart a doubt,
He raifes fuch a noife and rout!
To's trowel feet he points in fury,
Prefumptio juris et de jure.

His ftory credit gain'd with fome,
Others believ'd it all a hum.
The truth had ftill remain'd in doubt,
Had he not let the fecret out:

His vanity lent him a fling,
Nothing would ferve him but he'd fing;
He fung the fong that ftopt the Gauls
When clambering up the Roman walls.

BATHING MACHINE.

O CARRIAGE of amphibious nature!
Suited to ply by land and water,
And, like the crab, with backward pace,
Thy former track again to trace!
When to the founding fhore I go,
Snugly in thee myfelf I ftow,
As in the horfe the crafty Greek
When on old Troy he play'd a trick:
Than him I purpofe to do more;
He back'd by many a valiant fcore,
Did only plunder Neptune's town,
I'll buffet Neptune's felf alone.—

Oft have I wifh'd, and wifh'd again,
And found my wifhes ftill in vain,
When trundling along the fand,
To have a hold of Delia's hand :
Oft have I proffer'd up a prayer
Unto that goddefs wife and fair,
Who, for the fake of good example,
Chang'd Baucis' cot into a temple,
That fhe the only means would grant
Of making Delia's heart relent ;
That this fame jolting, juftling waggon,
In which fo clumfily I jog on,
She'd turn into a fplendid chariot,
Sole teft, in female eyes, of merit ;
That fhe would change this meagre hack,
Whofe ribs are fymbols of his rack,
(For all within's fo empty quite,
That thro' them you may fee the light)
And for the ftumbling fcarecrow brute
Four fiery fteeds would fubftitute :

Now, Delia, will you not confeſs,
That if thoſe things were brought to paſs,
Sans farther ſcruple you'd ſtep in
And fly with me to Gretna Green?

ON SEEING

SIR JAMIE

PURCHASE A JEST BOOK.

SAY, Mufe, (for well thou canft I wot)
What charm has loos'd the Gordian knot
Of Jamie's purfe, the fage profound,
In field and forum both renown'd,—
That purfe where captive fhillings pine,
Where copper fleeps as in the mine,
Unwak'd by Mifery's plaintive prayer:
Or, if a farthing 'fcape, 'tis rare.
Say, purfe, what could induce thy Lord
To draw a fhilling from his hoard?—
—Alas! poor gentleman! he's fmit
With paffion to be thought a wit,
But lacking brains that can fupply it,
He's forc'd, hard fate! he's forc'd to buy it.

GRETNA GREEN*.

NO more the foldier on the dewy turf,
With fhield-propt head, ftretches himfelf to reft;
Where once in furious fhock the battle clos'd,
Now rufh fond lovers into others arms;
Soft fighs are heard where erft the trumpet blew;
The field of Mars is now the bed of love.
No more "the armourers accomplifhing the knights
" With bufy hammers clofing rivets up,
" Give dreadful note of preparation."
Far other arts the fon of Vulcan plies;
To rivet clofe the indiffoluble chain,
To beat the fpear into fweet Cupid's dart,
To fan Love's fires, to harnefs Venus' doves,—
Thefe are thy toils, great Prieft of Gretna Green.

* The place where the Scottifh army lay during the night before the
battle of Solway.

I

ADVICE TO THE BEE*.

MISTRESS Bee, when you hum, whether profe,
  whether lyrics,
Whether cynical fatires, or puff'd panegyrics,
Pitch nor high, nor too low, ftill avoid in your tones
Th' ill-nature of wafps, and the dulnefs of drones.

* A Periodical Poblication under that Title.

THE

POETS' LAST WILL AND TESTAMENT;

OR, A

DIALOGUE WITH THE NOTARY.

P. SINCE Death, I now fee, will grant no reprieve,
To the *heirs of my body* my fubftance I leave
In equal proportions. N. Your fubftance! good Sir;
I never —but where is it?—pray tell me where?
And as for your heirs, I have fure been in bad luck,
For I thought you had none procreated in wedlock.
P. My fubftance, d'ye fee Sir, 's thefe bones and
      this fkin,
And tho' heirs I've had none, or in wedlock, or fin;
Tho' none I have had *matrimonio ftante*,
Of *pofthumous* ones in the grave I'll have plenty.

Q. F. F. Q. S.

CLOACINA'S COMPLAINT

то

THE COLLEGE OF CLUTHA.

IN other Temples, lo, the tapers' ray
Makes midnight almoſt emulate the day;
Ev'n private ſhrines the nightly lamp illumes,
And oily incenſe drowns mephitic fumes,—
Witneſs that ſacred dome, ſo fine, where JOHN,
Seated with breeches off, yea, And arſe on,
Ponders and pores o'er many a learned Work,
Reads THOMAS PAINE, and tears poor EDMUND
BURKE.

But to my theme—Soon as the wint'ry Sun,
His race nigh finifh'd ere 'tis well begun,
Sinks down to reft amidft the Atlantic wave,
Here darknefs drear as in Cimmerian cave
Prevails. And, tho' 'tis chief at morning hour
My vot'ries come their orifons to pour,
Yet hither too fome pious fouls repair
To join with bended knee in evening pray'r:
Then, ah! too oft the offerings, that are paid,
Not on my altar but my throne are laid.
Ev'n Porcus felf, tho' provident he keeps
A lantern burning, even while he fleeps,
Not *retro* in his poop but in his *roftrum*,
Like Bardolph's,—or as if 'twere ftung by *æftrum*,—
Ev'n he (for oft this lamp of his untrimm'd
Sheds " a *religious* light," by *fnuff* bedimm'd)
Ev'n Porcus felf with many a grunt and figh
Commits miftakes, and leaves my fhrine a *fly*.
But 'tis not on my own account alone
That this moft juft complaint I here propone,

Nor is it with intention to befpatter
My honour'd, venerable Alma Mater,
But (Jove *juvante*) all to put a ftop
To thofe mifhaps, which they who hither grope,
Oft meet withal.   For who can unconcern'd
Behold a youth, with gown and hofe well darn'd,
(*Feftina lente* quite forgotten in
His hurry) fall, and cut both hofe and fhin?—
Miftake his exercife for taylor's bill,—
Or 'ftead of Homer tear his F——y H—ll,—
Or make *Meanderings of Fancy* kifs
His breech—inftead of *Cafus Principis :*
('Twas darknefs thus made Jacob in idea
Kifs Rachel, while he kifs'd the blear'd-eyed Leah.)
O then, may you, to whom the power pertains
Of hindering fuch mifhaps, lift to my ftrains;
A fuppliant Deity, O view with pity,
Who afks— not tapers dipt in fpermaceti,
Who afks no patent lamp, no waxen light,
But, or—fuch oil as Lufs's thrifty Knight

In drops, like laud'num, on his fallad fprinkles,—
Or—farthing candle, fuch as dimly twinkles
In's bottle, never turn'd to other ufe,
Save when it holds the currant's vinous juice,
Juice which doth gripe his Knightfhip's guts full fore,
But other guts, not feafon'd to it, more,
Juice which, I pray, may be the mortal dofe
Of all who thefe my juft demands oppofe.

CLOACINA.

Cluthæ. Pridie. Id. Dec.
Anno Salutis, MDCCXCIII.

JUS DIVINUM.

Where is there to be found a fool fo arrant,
As to deny that I'm the Lord's vicegerent?
For who can fay that e'er I have been flack,
To burn, rob, murder, *ravifh*, hew, and hack?
Who is there dares my regal right to doubt,
But trembles for Siberia or the knout,
Proving I am, the juft, the mild, the good,
The Lord's anointed—with my hufband's blood?

KATHERINE.

ENGLAND'S FAITHFULNESS

TO HER FAITHFUL ALLIES;

OR,

THE MONOPOLY OF THE RIVER SCHELDT SUPPORTED.

T HEIR *High Mynheerſhips*, thriftier far than we,
Their *water* keep ſafe under *lock* and *key;*
While—to defend it, and its ſhores of mud,
We, fools, expend a *Zuyder Zea* of blood.

K

A

GENTLE EMETIC,

OR

A CONJUGAL SALUTE BY A JOVIAL WIFE.

T HE patience of Socrates ne'er was fo tried,
As was Sneakum's by his dearer half;
The Sage's fpoufe emptied a *pot* on his head,
Poor Sneakum's, more *Liberal,—herfelf*

TO

LUCINDA ABSENT,

OR,

THE MIRACULOUS MAGNET.

THIS Magnet, fpite of nature's laws,
Still as more diftant ftronger draws,
And what's more ftrange, (too well I feel!)
Attracts all hearts but hearts of fteel.

LADIES OF EDINBURGH.

DIRECTIONS FOR A WINDY DAY.

Fair ladies, when the winds blow high,
And mark the finely rounded thigh,
Be sure pull on your silken hose,
If you would wish to please the beaux.
Haste, reef the petticoat amain,
And tuck up tight the flowing train:
Take care to fasten firm the wig,
Lest in the air it dance a jig.
Then sally forth with pointed toe;
Invoke the friendly blast to blow:
" Thrice happy gales," your lovers cry out,
" That thus luxuriously riot,
" Amidst the charms of nymphs so coy,
" And towzle while we dare not toy."

DESPAIR.

(BY A DUTCH LOVER.)

THIS Stream flow winding thro' the *fragrant*
    bogs,
With murmurs not its own,—but of its frogs,
(Fair am'rous frogs, that *fing* * their croaking loves
In notes more fweet than notes of cooing doves)
This Stream,—I vow,—ne'er ruffled by a wave,
Shall be my death; the mud below—my grave.

    * Antiquam in limo ranæ *cecinere* querelam.
                              VIRG.

HARP.

THE captive Ifraelites of old,
(As we in Holy Writ are told)
Forgetting Sion's flats and fharps,
Dejected hung their ufelefs harps
The weeping willow trees upon,
Faſt by the ſtreams of Babylon.
So I, an exile from thy fight,
In drooping doleful piteous plight,
Have laid at reſt my tunelefs tongue,
And my harfh harp on willow hung,
In hopes that Zephyr's downy wings,
Sweeping gently o'er the ſtrings,

Softer plainings forth may fend

Than thofe of my unfkilful hand,

And, partial to th' Æolian note,

O'er beds of flowers may with it float

To thee, and light the latent fire,

Which rougher gales would make expire.

But if the fofteft melting airs,

Which Zephyr on his pinions bears,

Thy heart fhould rather cool than warm,

And, like my freezing notes, do harm ;

If difappointment or fufpenfe

Should ftill point to fome future hence,

Sufpended on the branch with me

Sweet harp, O fing my elegy!

ON SEEING

A LADY DROP HER GARTER.

I'D not change place with Prince or King,
Or any such poor paultry thing;
No,—could I this fad being barter,
O that I were that happy garter!
More boldly then I'd prefs my plea,
And, 'ftead of kneeling, clafp thy knee.

TO

A LADY

WHO LENT ME HER FAN DURING A STORM OF LIGHTNING.

FAIR nymph, a ſtranger all unknown
Would bleſs thee for thy charming loan;
But, ah ! he feels the lightning's gleams
Are far leſs dangerous than the beams
     Of thy bright eye.

L

APOLOGY

TO THE SAME·LADY

FOR ALLOWING HER FAN TO BE WET BY THE RAIN.

How many thoufands of ill-fated
Wretches have their ruin dated
From gifts or loans! A *non pareille*
Was th' caufe why father Adam fell.
Great Hercules his death-blow got
By putting on a gifted coat.
Poor Phaeton danc'd a headlong jig
For borrowing his father's Gig.
Troy, proof againft all human force,
Blazed round Minerva's hobby horfe:
To me a Fan had done the fame,
Had blown my heart into a flame,

While Cupid, 'mongſt the radii hid,

With darts the conflagration fed :—

What could I,— then,—but what I have done?

What elſe in ſuch caſe would have ſaved one?

What— but drench the Urchin's wing?

What, but wet his founding ſtring?

IMPROVEMENT

ON THE ART OF

POETRY,

SUGGESTED AND EXEMPLIFIED.

RHYME fhould not be degraded fo as to

Chime on the fyllable laft of the verfe :

Surè, if to fet your beft foot foremoft be

Tour rule in th' art of life—why not in this?

LET others praife with ill-coin'd lies
The *brightnefs* of their fair one's eyes,
To thine, fweet Lady, I'll be jufter,
Their very *darknefs* is their luftre.
Ev'n in the fable gloom of night,
Like grimalkin's, the ftartled fight
They ftrike, or as the fkin of whiting
Stuck on the wall poor imps to frighten.
In fhort, fo piercing is their ray,
I wonder how in mirror they
Themfelves can view; or how th' reflection,
Don't fpoil your matchlefs fair complection;
Or how, when hearts are fcorch'd to cinders,
Your looking-glafs don't fly to flinders.

ON THE

DEATH

OF A

LADY.

" Ah flore venuſtatis abrepta !"

DEATH poized his dart with ſlow protracted
    aim :
With look ſerene her fate LUCINDA viewed ;
She, beauteous flower, ſmiled drooping o'er the
    ſtream
Which undermined her root,—ſmiled, for ſhe ſaw
Heaven cloudleſs pictured in the cryſtal flood.

CLEMENCY.

And Pharoah hardened his heart at this time also, neither would he let the people go. Exodus c. viii. v. 32.

THE ruffian Murderer is fentenc'd to die,

And Slavery's profcribed by the general cry;

But a junto ufurping the national powers,

While the nation moft meanly, moft abjectly cowrs,

Grants a refpite of four years—to cool the *mad*

   fever,—

Then, bolder become,—a free pardon for ever.

IMITATIONS AND TRANSLATIONS.

M

EPISTOLA

AD TORQUATUM.

Hor. Lib. I. Epiſt. v.

SI potes archaicis conviva recumbere lectis,

Nec modicâ cœnare times olus omne patellâ ;

Supremo te ſole domi, Torquate, manebo.

Vina bibes iterum Tauro diffuſa, paluſtres

Inter Minturnas Sinueſſanumque Petrinum.

Sin melius quid habes, arceſſe ; vel imperium fer.

IMITATED.

GIF an auld timmer-bottom'd chair
Your doup can thole, and gif for fare
Ye wad na think yourfel far wrang
Wi' a farle 'noth a roafted whang,
Till gloamin time at hame I'll wait,
In hopes that ye'll come o'er the gate.
I'll gie you drink your craig to kittle,
That's eilans wi' the loufy title,
Coft by that fcat-necked loun,
Kent by the name o' CLERK — —.
But gin ye like fome ither kind,
Ye've naething but to fpeak your mind.

Jamdudum fplendet focus, & tibi munda fupellex.

Mitte leves fpes, & certamina divitiarum,

Et Mofchi caufam., cras nato Cæfare feftus

Dat veniam fomnumque dies : impunè licebit

Æftivam fermone benigno tendere noctem.

Quò mihi fortuna, fi non conceditur uti?

Parcus ob heredis curam, nimiumque feverus,

Affidet infano. potare et fpargare flores

Incipiam, patiarque vel inconfultus haberi.

Quid non ebrietas defignat ? operta recludit,

My ingle's bleezing unco canty;
My plenifhing's fu clean and dainty.
Lay by a' thought now for a wee,
And think na o' the penny fee.
The morn, ye ken, 's a hauliday,
And we may either fleep or play.
Wi' cracks the time till braid day-light,
Will feem as fhort's a fimmer night.

What needs I care for gear and gowd,
Unlefs to ufe them I'm allow'd?
Wha, for the fake o' his neift heir,
Keeps his ain wame tume, fcrimp, and bare,
And feeds upon the hufk and hule,
Is juft the neift bore to a fool.
I'll now begin to drink and fing,
My pen I'll in the ingle fling;
I care na tho' wi' girnin chaft
The warl a' fou'd ca' me daft.

Ken ye o' ought drink canna do?—
The clofeft hunks whan he is fou

Spes jubet effe ratas, ad prœlia trudit inertem,
Solicitis animis onus eximit, addocet artes.
Fecundi calices quem non fecere difertum?
Contractâ quem non in paupertate folutum?

Hæc ego procurare & idoneus imperor, & non
Invitus; ne turpe toral, ne fordida mappa
Corruget narcs; ne non & cantharus, & lanx
Oftendat tibi te: ne fidos inter amicos
Sit, qui dicta foras eliminet; ut coeat par, -
Jungaturque pari. Brutum tibi, Septimiumque,

Speaks out his mind;—drink realizes
Our hopes and wiffes; and it heezes
The coward's fwitherin heart to fecht:
Frae aff the mind it lifts the weight
O' ilka care; in ilka art ·
It learns a man to play his part.
Wha, whan h' as taen his proper tift,
Was ever kent to want the gift
O's gab? what puir man whan he's tozy,
But fpends as he ware bein and cozy.

Ye need na tell me to tak care,
To hae the buirdclaith clean and fair:
To hae the difhes glancin a'
That they yourfel to you may fhaw;
And no to bid 'mang friens wh'are merry
Folk wha wad clepe things to the Shirra,
Or chiels wha think that they are great,
Becaufe they hae a great eftate.

Et, nifi cœna prior, potiorque puella Sabinum
Detinet, affumam. locus eft & pluribus umbris :
Sed nimis arcta premunt olidæ convivia capræ.

Tu, quotus effe velis, refcribe ; et rebus omiffis
Atria fervantem poftico falle clientem.

Ye'll meet wi' —— and wi' ——,
And ——, unlefs fome laffie ——
Or ither tryft (the Deil ———
And ony thing that hauds a —— ——)
Keep him awa.   Attour ye've leave
To bring a frien or twa i' your fleeve.
But mind whan fok o'er clofe ye ftech,
It fometimes gars them fweat and pech.

Write me how mony ye're to bring :
Your caigh and care ahint you fling ;
And, while puir bodies *on the row,*
I' th' kitchen ftan their cuds to chow,
Steal out and never fafh your pow.

N

AD VIRGILIUM.

Hor. carm. lib. 4. Od. 12.

Jam veris comites, quæ mare temperant,
Impellunt animæ lintea Thraciæ :
Jam nec prata rigent, nec fluvii ftrepunt
    Hiberna nive turgidi.
Nidum ponit, Ityn flebiliter gemens,   5
Infelix avis, et Cecropiæ domus
Æternum opprobrium ; quod male barbaras
    Regum eft ulta libidines.

HORACE.

ODE 12. BOOK 4.

THE weftlin wind, the Springtime's crony,
Now fkiffs alang the fea fae bonny,
And fills ilk fail. Now Crummie's cloots
Dent a' the lone : now to the coots
In meadow lawn, umquhile fae hard,
Ye'll fink, and ablins will be lair'd :
The burns, wi' fnaw brie fill'd, nae mair
Rufh, roarin like the Bars o' Ayr.
The Swallow now, puir fingin forner,
Clags up her neft i' th' winnock corner :
Welcome fhe is to ilka houfe,
Exceptin his, the blafted Loufe *,
Wha 'rave her wark o' mony a day,
In vengeance 'caufe fhe ftaw his ftrae.

* Corrupted perhaps from *Lufs*.

Dicunt in tenero gramine pinguium

Cuftodes ovium carmina fiftula;

Delectantque Deum, cui pecus et nigri   10

     Colles Arcadiæ placent.

Adduxere fitim tempora, Virgili;

Sed preffum Calibus ducere Liberum

Si geftis, juvenum nobilium cliens,   15

     Nardo vina merebere.

Nardi parvus onyx eliciet cadum,

Qui nunc Sulpitiis accubat horreis,

Spes donare novas largus, amaraque

     Curarum eluere efficax.   20

The Shepherd, tether'd to the braes
O' black Lochaber, fweetly plays,
To his lean flock, a highland fpring,
(Sic as auld OSSIAN ance did fing,)
Ilk han' by turns, wi' motion quick,
Now the fiddle, now the fiddle-ftick.

This heat gies ane a drouth, my frien,
Sae gif to lay your lugs ye green
In lochs o' punch, tak tent to hae
Twa lemons in your pouch,—or mae:
A pouchfu's able to wyle out,
Frae th' awmry neuk, my graybeard ftout
And fonfy, fitted weel to brew
In your funk faul hope ever new:
For fynin down, it's unco rare,
The bitter wagang o' ilk care.

Ad quæ fi properas gaudia, cum tua
Velox merce veni : non ego te meis
Immunem meditor tingere poculis,

  Plena dives ut in domo.

Verum pone moras et ftudium lucri ;   25
Nigrorumque memor, dum licet, ignium,
Mifce ftultitiam confiliis brevem :

  Dulce eft defipere in loco.

Hafte ye, and dinna fwitherin ftan,

But linkin tak your fit i' your han ;

And dinna in your hafte forget

To bring the Uncos pipin het.

Tell us how our auld Frien's the ——

Stan' 'gainft the warl croufe and ftainch,

And how the bonny Fernig foichals

Gie G — —n thieves and flaves their dichals :

I'm no for letting ye, ye fee,

(As I ware rich) gang lawin free.

Awa wi' teaglin, and the euk

O' ftappin mair in your poke neuk :

And now *forget*, as lang's ye dow,

Memento mori, and Death's pow :

Seafon your wifdom, now and than,

W'a curn o' folly i' the pan :

Truft me wha'm growin auld and keifint,

That weeltimed daffin's unco pleafant.

AD LIBRUM SUUM.

Hor. Epift. 20. Lib. 1.

Vertumnum Janumque, liber, fpectare videris;
Scilicet ut proftes Sofiorum pumice mundus.
Odifti claves, et grata figilla pudico :
Paucis oftendi gemis, et communia laudas ;
Non ita nutritus.. Fuge quo defcendere geftis :   5
Non erit emiffo reditus tibi.   Quid mifer egi ?
Quid volui ? dices, ubi quid te læferit ; et fcis
In breve te cogi, cum plenus languet armator.

TO

HIS BOOK.

Y E'VE now begun to caſt ſheeps een
At yon Beuk Shop; and in caufs ſkin,
Forſuith, wi' buirds gilt, ſheen, and braw,
Ye're unco fain yourſel to ſhaw.

Locks, coffers, keys and kiſts ye hate,
And whate'er pleaſes ane that's blate:
And yawmer 'cauſe ye're no allow'd
To mix amang the dinſome crowd,—
No ſae brought up.   E'en gang your wa,
But mind there nae return ava.

I've won myſel a bonny pirn,
Ye'll ſay, whan critics gybe and girn,
Or whan the reader, gauntin elf,
Chirts you into the crowded ſhelf,
Neiſt bletherin BURKE, the Windſor ſentry,
Wha' ſang the Gauls were in the entry *.

O

* Atque hic *auratis* volitans *argenteus* anſer
Porticibus, *Gallos* in limine adeſſe canebat.   VIRG. Æn. 8.

Quod fi non odio peccantis defipit augur,

Carus eris Romæ, donec te deferat ætas.   10

Contrectatus ubi manibus fordefcere vulgi

Cœperis; aut tineas pafces taciturnus inertes,

Aut fugies Uticam, aut vinctus mitteris Ilerdam.

Ridebit monitor non exauditus; ut ille,

Qui male parentem in rupes protrufit afellum   15

Iratus.   Quis enim invitum fervare laboret?

Hoc quoque te manet, ut pueros elementa docentem

Occupet extremis in vicis balba feneftus.

Now, gif the greatnefs o' your faut
Wad let me fpae what's to come o't,—
To th' Lan' o' Cakes ye will be dear
Nae mair than for fome twa three year:
Belyve the creifhy croud will haunle
Your page, and foil't : ablins fome caunle
Doup ye maun kifs, (far better that,
Than do the fame to Lords, I wat :)
Whatreks! puir, unkent, cowrin finner,
Some lazy moths will mak their dinner
Upon your leaves : or elfe may be
Twa baubees worth o' fnuff or tea
Ye're doom'd to fwathe. I in my fleeve
Will laugh fu' hearty whan ye grieve,
And fay (like him wha on a day
His crofs-grain'd afs fhot o'er the brae,
On feein' that he could na ftop her)
Wha will to Couper will to Couper.
Forby a' that ;—haverin Auld Age,
Pointin. alang your title page,
Will ding, wi meikle dule and wae,
Into puir gets, the A, B, C.

Cum tibi fol tepidus plures admoverit aures,

Me libertino natum patre, et in tenui re   20

Majores pennas nido extendiffe loqueris ;

Ut quantum generi demas, virtutibus addas :

Me primis urbis belli placuiffe domique ;

Corporis exigui, præcanum, folibus aptum,

Irafci celerem, tamen ut placabilis effem.   25

In winter whan the bleezin ingle.

Draws round it fouk to hear your jingle,

Tell them, that I hae fcarce a gill;

O' gentle bluid for kings to fpill:

Tell that, in place o' the goofe pen

Ufed by my forbears, I hae taen

A pouk o' Pegafus's wing,

On whilk heez'd up I fcove and fing, ·

Sae, as ye ftow the ftunted tree,

That puddock-ftool my pedigree,

A branch o' laurel ye may eik.

Tell them, too, how I never feek

To fleech and pleafe the rich or great.

O' th' outward man I neift maun treat:

Say, then, I am a lang black chiel

Twa·ell amaift frae head to heel.

Afore the time I'm fome thocht gray

And lyart.   In a funny day

I like to beik.   Wi' fudden low

My anger's juft a tap o' tow;

Forte meum fi quis te percontabitur ævum ;

Me quater undenos fciat impleviffe Decembres,

Collegam Lepidum quo duxit Lollius anno.

But foon gaes out.   Gif fouk foud fpier
How auld I am; tell them,—that year
Whan daft Britannia turn'd knight errant,
An' fee't that loun S———'s tyrant
To fer' himfel, I was juft then
Maift four times twa, and twa times ten.

SAPHO TO PHAON.

AGNOVI preffas noti mihi cefpitis herbas:

De noftro curvum pondere gramen erat.

Incubui, tetigique locum qua parte fuifti;

Grata prius lacrymas combibit herba meas.

TRANSLATED BY AN ENGLISHMAN.

HERE the prefs'd herbs with bending tops betray,

Where oft entwin'd in am'rous folds we lay;

I kifs the earth which was once prefs'd by you,

And all with tears the with'ring herbs bedew.

POPE.

BY A SCOTCHMAN.

" FERVIDUM INGENIUM SCOTORUM."

THE fnows (no longer virgin fnows) betray

Where oft entwined in am'rous folds we lay;,

I kifs the place which once was prefs'd by you,

And all with tears the melting wreaths bedew.

EPIGRAMMA

G. BUCHANANI.

QUI te videt beatus eft,
  Beatior qui te audiet,
  Qui bafiat femideus eft,
    Qui te potitur eft Deus.

▶▶▶▶▶◀◀◀◀◀

HAPPY is he who fees thee fweetly fmile,
Happier who hears the mufic of thy voice,
A demi-god is he who kiffeth thee,
Who clafps thee yielding in his arms—a God.

P

VERSES

IN

LATIN.

" Ifta tamen mala funt : quafi nos manifefta negemus ;
" Hæc mala funt : fed tu non meliora facis."

Mart. lib. 2. Ep. 8.

——— ——————Vetuit me tale voce Quirinus
Poft mediam nocteni vifus ubi fomnia vera.

HOR.

THE

MUSE's PRELIMINARY EXPOSTULATION

AND

ADVICE.

To print or not my Latin verfes?
I afk'd the Mufe; quoth fhe, " Moft arfes
" (The feat of *Englifh* judgment) are
" Become fo nice, you may defpair
" To pleafe in Englifh, or in Latin,
" Unlefs your paper's foft as fatin.
" But why this jargon—*cur Latina?*
" Whence comes this *rabies canina?*

" 'Tis fure at beſt a fooliſh freak,

" To chuſe to bark, when you can ſpeak.

" Well then, if you'll take my advice,

" The *actual cautery* to each place

" That bears of canine jaw the trace,"—

" Alas," I ſtopt her, " would you bid

" M' incur the guilt of fuicide ?

" Would y'ave me turn *felo de ſe*,

" And light up an *auto-da-fe*

" Of my dear ſelf, like Indian relicts,

" Where widowhood's held worſt of delicts ?

" No,—I reject your harſh preſcription,

" For if, t' each place of the deſcription,

" Which you have given, 'twere applied,

" From cap-à-pe I ſhould be fried.

PORCUS ᴇᴛ ACHATES,

CARMEN PASTORALE-ELEGIACUM,

MEMORIÆ SACRUM

R O B I N I,

CAMERARUM ET IGNIUM CUSTODIS,

IN COLLEGIO CLUTHÆ.

ACCESSERUNT NOTÆ SELECTISSIMÆ VARIORUM.

———

ADITIO NOVA, PRIORIBUS AUCTIOR ET EMENDATIOR, ET MULTIS
MACULIS EXPURGATA.

Q

PORCUS ET ACHATES.

FORTE ſub anguſto *Jani* confederat antro
Gruntator Porcuſve, atque umbra fidelis Achates;
Ambo florentes roſtris, ac Arcades ambo,
Et potare pares, et reſpondere parati.

NOTÆ.

1. *Anguſto Jani antro.* Taberna
ſcilicet Janitoris, ad Januam publi-
cam ſita, et ideo, et quia oſtia ejus
contra certamina Bacchi nunquam
clauſa funt, antrum Jani hic appellata.
Heinſius.

2. *Umbra.* Umbra eſt amicus vel
comes inferior, cui nomen datum, ex
eo quod aliam ad convivium ſequere-
tur velut umbra corpus. Vid. Hor.
Sat. lib. 2. ſat. 8. v. 22. *Heinſius.*

3. *Roſtris.* Naſis rubicundis. *Bro-
dæus.*

Arcades. De hoc verbo mag-
num eſt certamen inter interpre-
tes. Alii aſſerunt, poetam ad Arcades paſtores alludere, quia paſtores
ſemper fuerunt cultores Veneris, et
potores quoque myrtum Veneris
cum vite Bacchi haud raro jungunt.
Nonnulli magis ſubtiliores, *Arcades*

in hoc loco ex *arcu* cœleſti ſeu Iride
derivant, quia, ut dicunt, ſicut nubes
pluviis gravata onus demittit et Iri-
dem ſæpe oſtentat, ita Diſcipulus
Bacchi e ſtomacho nimium repleto
numen ejicit, *arcum* quodammodo Iridi
ſimilem exhibens; cui verba poetæ ap-
plicari poſſint;

" *Mille trahens varios adverſo ſole
colores.*"

Fulta eſt præterea hæc opinio auc-
toritate poetæ noſtratis, cujus verba
concinna, tametſi vernacula, cum ve-
nia eruditorum, citabo. *Pinkertonius.*

" Ganc out to piſh in gutters thick
Some fell and fome gaed rockin;
Sawny hang fneerin on his ſtick
To ſee bauld Hutchin bockin
Rainbows that day."

Chriſt Kirk on the Green. Canto 3.

Pocula, heu ! flentes, mœrentia pocula mifcent,   5
Queftibus et Robini alternis funera lugent :
Alternis igitur contendere verfibus ambo
Coepere ; alternos Mufæ meminiffe volebant.
Hos Porcus, tum illos referebat in ordine Achates.

Porc. Fundite lamenta et fufpiria rauca Togati, 10
Necnon vos qui fine togis vim frigoris audent ;
Nam tenebrofa eft omnino fcintillula Veftæ,
Pœnis atque Sacerdos terræ plectitur infons.

Togati. Toga eft habitus quorun-
dam in Collegio Cluthæ. Quidam
togis non induuntur.   *Lubin.*

12. *Scintillula Vefta.* Deæ Veftæ
facer erat ignis ; et *fcintillula Vefla* hic
ponitur pro ignibus vel focis Acade-
micis quos Robinus accendere et fo-
vere folebat, et qui, eo defuncto, fin-
guntur extincti.

13. *Pænis atque Sacerdos terræ plec-
itur infons.* In hifce verbis contine-
tur allufio elegantiffima pœnæ cui ob-
noxiæ erant Virgines Veftales quæ,
fi votum caftitatis violarent, vivæ fe-
peliebantur. Infons procul dubio e-
rat Robinus hujus criminis, nam nunquam fe voto caftitatis fubjiciebat, id-
circo nunquam reus ftare potuit iftius
voti violationis. Sed quamvis inno-
cuus effet fepulturam feu pœnam terræ paffus eft.   *Mackullæus.*

Ach. Fuſtim ex ilice ſectam, qua velut enſe corufco

Hortum cuſtodire folebas, abjice, David, 15

Ramum et mœſtum fume cupreſſi, nam tibi nulla

Mordentem *calefactum* dextera libera fundet,

14. *Fuſtim qua velut enſe corufco hortum cuſtodire folebas.* Cave, lector,
ne poetam hic arguas alicujus obſcœ-
næ alluſionis ad Deum Priapum qui
hortos cuſtodiebat, de quo Horatius,

———————" *fures dextra coercet*,
" *Obſcænoque ruber porrectus ab ingu-
ine palus*"
namque palus Davidis jamdudum
" *inutile lignum*" dici potuit. Sed fuſtis
feu baculus querceus, quem in ma-
nu gerebat, magnæ erat utilitatis ad
coercendum *profanum vulgus* [gallice
Sans Culottes, anglice *Swiniſ Multi-
tſde*, Scotice *Rabble*] quo minus hortum Academicum introiret. In hoc
verfu, igitur, facile patet, mentem
diviniorem Poetæ profpexiſſe ad hortum Paradifaicum, ubi enſis flammi-
ferus feu corufcus, regreſſum paren-
tam humani generis interpellabat.

Burlius quond. Rect. Magnif.

16. *Cupreſſi.* Cupreſſus arbos fu-

nerea mœrori facra. *Lub.*

17. *Mordentem calefactum dextera
libera fundet.* A *calefacio* derivatur
calefactum aliter *drachma*, per fynco-
pen *dram*, mutato *d* in *w*, et *r* poſito
inter *a* et *m Warm*, et cum articulo
præpoſito fecundum idioma Anglica-
num *a warm*, modus loquendi Cluthæ
frequenter uſitatus. Hanc folationem
et fugatorem frigoris ſimul ac cura-
rum, raro ſibi negabat Robinus; ſæpe
itidem Davidem ut particeps eſſet in-
vitabat. Hic loci ergo Poeta, miri-
fica arte, caufam monſtrat permag-
nam, oh quam luctus Davidis move-
ri debebat, caufam quidem aptiſſi-
mam, ſive fpectes ad perfonam quæ
loquitur, fcilicet umbram Achatem,
vel ad perfonam de qua loquitur, fcilicet umbram Davidem. *Idem.*

Mordentem. Nemo fere ignorat
calefactum leniter mordere et titillare
palatum. *Idem.*

Porc. Stirpe illuftri Dónaldfoná periit ortus !

Quifnam cautus, mane Hyberno, jam E—â inàulâ,

Lumina tondèbit, cum præbent languida lùcem, 20

Et titubantibus huc illuc duplicantur ocèllis !

---

18. *Stirpe illuftri Donaldfona.* Mater Robini foror erat Donaldfonii in-
clytæ mēmoriæ. Quas àures non
perculit fama Donaldfonii ? Sed Robini fama fois meritis nititur ;

Nām genus et proavos, et quæ non fe-
cimus ipfi,
Vix ea noftra vóco. Ov. *Burkius.*

20. *Lumina tóndebit.* Virtuté poe-
ticæ licentiæ hæc figura, ex alia claf-
fe matutina deducta, transfertur ad
claffem ——m, in hac enim Robinus lumina feu candelas tantum accendere, non tondere, folebat. *Id.*

21. *Et titubantibus buc illuc dupli-*
cantur ocellis. Nullus cultor Bacchi
ignorat lumina, five fint candelæ, five

ftellæ, five lunæ radii, five felis o-
culi, vifui ebrioforum duplicari. Sed
hic queftio oritur ; quomodo fit ut ille, cujus eft officium mores aliis ex-
ponere, mores fuos tantopere negligit?
Cave, lector, ne judicio tuo temere
utaris. Non equidem mores fuos negligit Porcus. Mores ftrenue docet
tam exemplo quam precepto. Nam
quid citius homines a vitio deterrere
poteft quam vultus ejus deformis. Si-
mili modo Spartani fervos ebriofos
derifui liberorum oftendere folebant.
Sed Porcus benignior feipfum devo-
vet exemplum fimulque victimam.

Heinfius.

Ach. Tale tuum carmen nobis, divine poeta,
Quale fopor feffis in templo, quale per æftum
Dulcis aquæ faliente fitim reftinguere rivo.

Porc. Pocula bina novo fpumantia *portra* quo-

tannis, 25

Craterafque duos ftatuam tibi mitis Henevæ:

---

22. *Divine poeta.* Hic Achates
amicum fuum et patronum adulatur.
Idem.

23. *Quale fopor feffis in templo.*
Nihil fane jucundius eft fopore feffis
in templo vel ecclefia, præfertim quando præfertim quando Porcus grun-
nitum monotonum mittit. Sed procul, o procul abfit ruditus ineptus
Afini Campfei. *Idem.*

24. *Dulcis aquæ.* Aquavitæ fcilicet.

Rivo pro fcypho ufurpatur.
Idem.

25. *Portra,* abjecto *a,* et inferto *e*
inter *t* et *r, Porter,* eft liquor ex brafio decoctus. *Portra* eft nomen inde-
clinabile tertiæ declinationis. *Burkius.*

26. *Tibi.* Robino fcilicet. *Hein.*

Henevæ. Heneva vel *Geneva,*
per contractionem *Gin,* liquor eft ex
brafio et juniperis decoctus, mictu-
ram valde promovens. *Idem.*

Et multo imprimis hilarans convivia Baccho,

Vina novum bibam calathis Ferntofia nectar.

Cantabunt mihi Damœtas et Lyctius Ægon :

Saltantes Satyros fimulabit Filleodæus.   30

Eheu! fed fonat hora infelix : nunc redeundum,

Officia ad *Ciceronis,*—peffima, peffima vappa!

---

28. *Ferntofia.* Ager Ferntofius, five Ferntofhius, fitus eft prope agrum Cullodenenfem, locum celeberrimum redditum a quo tempore Dux Cumbriæ victoriam gloriofam, fufis ibi Caledoniis barbaris, nactus eft. Narratio hujus victoriæ literis fanguineis fcribi debet; per fpatium enim octo dierum poft pugnam, quatuor millibus Scotorum à quindecim millibus Anglorum fuperatis, agri vaftabantur, tuguria igne cremabantur, virgines violabantur, homines nulla arma præter peda paftoria gentes, cum feminis et liberis, (proh nefas!) jugulabantur. O Gens Anglicana humaniffima, clementiffima! O immaculata ultrix fanguinis regii! nunquam veftris manibus trucidabatur

vel rex proprius, vel regina alienæ exul inops hofpes, vel hoftis magnanimus proditione captus,—non ;— Teftes funt mifericordiæ, juftitiæ, fideique Anglicanæ, Carolus, Maria, Vallas. O Gens mitiffima, Chriftianiffima, lumina ad Africam et Indiam vertite ; tunc, O Gens juftiffima, execrationes pias in fævitiam Gallicam eructato.   *Heinf.*

30. *Saltantes Satyros fimulabit Filleodæus.* In antiquis temporibus Sacerdotes fæpe faltabant, et aliquando reges pedes quaffare dignabantur. In exemplo erant Salii Sacerdotes inter Romanos, et inter Judæos David rex.
                                Idem.

32. *Officia ad Ciceronis.* Perlectio Ciceronis de Officiis. *Lubin.*

BALNEUM,

sive

MUNDITIES ANGLICANA.

" Quî fit, Balneolum, *gelidi* cui nomen adeptum,

" Nos ut decipias, lymphas reddafque tepentes?

" Quî fit, cum exuftus morientibus æftuat herbis

" Campus, ut haud alio tu tempore majus abundes?"

Talia tum mihi fcitanti vox redditur undis.

" Caufa eft hæc de qua quæris :—latices mihi nullos

" Suppeditant fontes, non ullos nubila cœli:

" Aft lymphas derivo omnes, a rore fluente,

" Exfudato illis qui me fuefcunt celebrare;

" Atque fcaturigines folæ, quas accipio ufquam,

" Lipporum de luminibus ftillæ riguæ funt."

R

─────────────

[*From Burns's Poems.*]

TO A

M O U S E,

ON TURNING HER UP IN HER NEST, WITH THE PLOUGH,
NOVEMBER 1785.

W EE, fleekit, cowrin, tim'rous beaftie,
O, what a panic's in thy breaftie!
Thou need na ftart awa fae hafty,
    Wi' bickering brattle;
I wad be laith to rin an' chafe thee,
    Wi' murd'ring *pattle.*

 I'm truly forry Man's dominion
Has broken Nature's focial union,
An' juftifies that ill opinion,
    Which makes thee ftartle
At me, thy poor, earth-born companion,
    An' *fellow-mortal!*

AD MUREM,

NIDIS ARATRO EVERSIS.

EHEU, parva nitedula, qualis nunc tremor implet
Pectora! ne fubitò celeri te proripe curfu ;
Infectari te nollem rullâ truculentâ.

Naturæ imperio humano fœdus fociale
Ruptum mî dolet, et juſtam me dicere cogit
Illam fufpicionem, qua fit ut exfilis a me
Terrigenâ comite, in terram tecum redituro.

I doubt na, whiles, but thou may thieve;
What then? poor beaſtie, thou maun live!
A *daimen icker* in a *thrave*

'S a ſma' requeſt.
I'll get a bleſſin wi' the lave,

An' never miſs't!

Thy wee bit *houſie*, too, in ruin!
It's ſilly wa's the win's are ſtrewin!
An' naething, now, to big a new ane,

O' foggage green!
An' bleak December's winds enſuin,

Baith ſnell and keen!

Haud equidem dubito quin tu furere aliquando.
Quidni? animal miferum, te certe vivere oportet.
Granum e mergite totâ, ecce petitio parva!
Grano a te fumpto, damnum haud dignofcere
    poffum;
Et mihi quod fupereft cœlo faufto fruar illo.

Angufta illa domus mœftam dat fracta ruinam;
Structuram invalidam fpectas difpergere ventos;
Nec virides ullas ftipulas, illam ad renovandam,
Ufquam fuppeditant arvà.   Interea imminet afper
Mordaces referens ventos acrefque December.

Thou faw the fields laid bare an' wafte,
An' weary Winter comin faft,
An' cozie here, beneath the blaft,

   Thou thought to dwell,
Till crafh! the cruel *coulter* paft

   Out thro' thy cell.

That wee bit heap o' leaves an' ftibble,
Has coft thee monie a weary nibble!
Now thou's turn'd out, for a' thy trouble,

   But houfe or hald,
To thole the Winter's fleety dribble,

   An' cranreuch cald!

But, Moufie, thou art no thy lane,
In proving *forefight* may be vain;
The beft laid fchemes o' *Mice* an' *Men*,

   Gang aft a-gley,
An' lea'e us nought but grief an' pain,

   For promis'd joy

Agros tu nudatos vâſtatoſque, hyememque
Vidiſti triſtem properantem ; ſpemque fovebas,
Obtecta hic ut contra aquilones degere poſſes ;
At ſcindit nidos crudeli vomere aratrum.

Congeries hæc culmorum exigua et foliorum,
Trito dente fuit, multo et convěcta labore ;
Nunc operam perdiſti, et tectis exul ademptis,
Frigus acerbum perferres pluviaſque nivales.

Sed non indicium tu, parva nitedula, ſola es,
Quam vana eſt mens prudens et præſaga futuri :
Conſiliis, quæ muribus et mortalibus ægris
Arte ineuntur ſummâ, haud raro caſus iniquus
Accidit : et, ſperatæ lætitiæ vice, crebrò
Nil inventum eſt præter triſtitiam atque dolorem.

Still thou art bleft, compar'd wi' *me!*
The prefent only toucheth thee:
But, Och! I backward caft my e'e
     On profpects drear!
An' forward, tho' I canna *fee,*
      I *guefs* an' *fear!*

Attamen haud incertum eſt, præ me te eſſe beatum ;

Hora etenim præſens ſolùm te tangere poſſit ;

Quum retro, inque dies mœſtos mea lumina verto,

Et quamvis non prævideo, auguror atque tremiſco.

S

NOTES.

[P. 38. *Fragments* of a Poem on Duelling.]

From motives of prudence I have been induced to suppress several things which I had some thoughts of publishing. Of others I have published fragments only,—trusting that the *disjecti membra poetæ* may still be found.—

——————————————*O ubi* illa priorum
Scribendi quodcumque animo flagrante liberet
Simplicitas, cujus non audeo dicere nomen!

Juv. Sat. 1. lib. 1. v. 151.

[P. 50. On D——d H——e.]

My opinion of D——d H——e,—(what arrogance! exclaim his worshippers) my opinion of D——d H——e is not singular. See *Miscellanies in Prose and Verse* by the late Lord Gardenstone. But I cannot refrain from quoting the following passage from that work.

" His lively periods may procure
   Attention to the end of time ;
But will the world for such a lure,
   Forget chicanery's a crime ?
This prince of sceptics scarce could tell,
Why *china* shiver'd when it fell !

A Bacon's, Dryden's, Shakespeare's praise,
   He weakly tries to undermine ;
And, brilliant Martial to debase,
   Pretends he punn'd in every line ;
O'erlooks the great Preceptor's claims,
Yet strives to compliment his ideot pupil James,

Behold this precious sage advise
   Each peevish fool to cut his throat !
And deeds of infamy disguise
   Coligni's murder rivals not !
Then see him scruple to decide
Why Pym harrangued, or Hampden died.

Ye facred and immortal names,
  Which Freedom's fons with reverence hear,
When fophiftry your worth defames
  And toils to taint the public ear,
With what indignity and fcorn
  Ought fuch a libel to be torn !"
                    Sketches of celebrated characters, &c.

          And elfewhere
If * * * * has told ten thoufand Tory lies,
His faithlefs page take courage and defpife.
                    Mifcellanies, &c. p. 202.
          See alfo Haley.

[P. 70.]

His breech inftead of, &c.
Si quis erat dignus defcribi quod malus aut *fur.*
                    Hor. Sat. 4. *lib.* I. *v.* 3.
The man who converts the refearches and labours of others
to his own profit, is furely *dignus defcribi.*

[P. 78.]

The captive Ifraelites, &c. I meant thefe as burlefque verfes ;
but I begin to be afraid that their fcope may appear fomewhat
ambiguous. In fhort, I ftand in the predicament of the poor
painter, who found it neceffary to write under a picture, in
which he meant to reprefent a horfe,—*This is a horfe.*

[P. 89.]

Imitations and Tranflations. I am fenfible that this title is
ill-chofen. *Parodies* would have been a more fuitable one.

[P. 97.]

On the row. Such poor perfons as are found entitled to have
their caufes carried on *gratis* are faid to be *admitted to the benefit
of the Poors roll,* or *lift,*—or in old technical language to be upon *the row,* i. e. *the roll.*——This excellent inftitution is not in
every cafe, carried into execution in that confcientious manner
which " *the caufe of him who hath none to help him*" demands.

[P. 128.]

Agri vaſtabantur, &c. The truth of the repreſentation here given, is ſupported by the teſtimony of Smollet, in his poem entitled, *The Tears of Scotland.* I truſt that the following quotation, from that poem, will not be unwelcome to any Scotchman, or to any man of a liberal mind.

> " Yet, when the rage of battle ceas'd,
> The victor's ſoul was not appeas'd :
> The naked and forlorn muſt feel
> Devouring flames, and murdering ſteel.

> " The pious mother doom'd to death,
> Forſaken, wanders o'er the heath,
> The bleak wind whiſtles o'er her head,
> Her helpleſs orphans cry for bread ;
> Bereft of ſhelter, food and friend,
> She views the ſhades of night deſcend,
> And, ſtretch'd beneath th' inclement ſkies,
> Weeps o'er her tender babes, and dies.

> " Whilſt the warm blood bedews my veins,
> And unimpair'd remembrance reigns,
> Reſentment of my country's fate
> Within my filial breaſt ſhall beat ;
> And, ſpite of her inſulting foe,
> My ſympathiſing verſe ſhall flow,
> " Mourn, hapleſs Caledonia, mourn
> " Thy baniſh'd peace, thy laurels torn."

[P. 128.]

Filleodaeus. Callidus, quicquid placuit doloſo
    Condere furto.   Hor.
Vid. Note on p. 70.

[P. 131.]

Nitedula—rulla. Think not, O Critic, that thoſe two words, which, perhaps, thou may'ſt not have met with in the courſe of thy reading, are not *claſſical.* If thou art in doubt, conſult thy Dictionary.

FINIS.